CLASSIC
Desserts
HOME COOKING

D1472852

Publications International, Ltd.
Favorite Brand Name Recipes at www.fbnr.com

Pictured on the front cover: Mixed Berry Pie *(page 8).*

ISBN: 0-7853-7805-7

Manufactured in China.

8 7 6 5 4 3 2 1

Microwave Cooking: Microwave ovens vary in wattage. Use the cooking times as guidelines and check for doneness before adding more time.

CONTENTS

Chocolate Hazelnut Pie *(page 15)*

Orange Cappuccino Brownies *(page 34)*

Spiced Pear Tart *(page 50)*

CLASS NOTES

A fabulous dessert adds a special touch to any meal and this collection is sure to please. You'll marvel at the variety of desserts—cakes, pies, cookies and mousses—and the multitude of flavors, such as vanilla, caramel, cherry, apple, berry, maple and, of course, chocolate!

Success in the kitchen is often achieved through careful organization and preparation. Before you begin a recipe, carefully read through the instructions, then gather all the ingredients and equipment. Do not make ingredient substitutions unless specifically called for in the recipe. Substitutions can alter the delicate balance of ingredients and the result may be less than perfect. Mastering the following skills will help ensure success in dessert-making every time.

BAKING TIPS

- Measure all ingredients carefully and accurately. To measure flour, spoon it lightly into a dry measuring cup and level it off with a straight-edge metal spatula (do not shake it down or tap it on the counter).

- Use the pan size specified in each recipe and prepare the pan as stated. The wrong size pan may cause the dessert to burn on the edges and bottom or sink in the middle.

- Oven temperatures may vary, so watch your dessert carefully and check for doneness using the test given in the recipe.

PASTRY MAKING TIPS

- Cut the shortening, margarine or butter into the flour and salt using a pastry blender or two knives until the mixture forms pea-sized pieces. Add the liquid, 1 tablespoon at a time, tossing lightly with a fork, until the dough is just moist enough to hold together when pressed.

- If the dough is sticky and difficult to handle, refrigerate it until firm. The easiest way to roll out pastry dough without sticking is to use a rolling pin cover and pastry cloth. Lightly flour the covered rolling pin and pastry cloth before using, and handle the dough quickly. A tough pie crust is the result of too much flour worked into the dough or overhandling.

- Roll the dough out to a $\frac{1}{8}$-inch-thick circle at least 1 inch larger than an inverted pie plate. To transfer dough to pie plate, place the rolling pin on one side of the dough. Gently roll the dough over the rolling pin once. Carefully lift the rolling pin and the dough, unrolling the dough over the pie plate. Ease the dough into the pie plate with fingertips and gently press into place. Be careful not to pull or stretch the dough, as this will cause it to shrink during baking.

- Often a pie crust is "baked blind," which means it is baked before the filling is added. To keep the pastry from puffing up during baking, line the crust with foil and fill it with dried beans, uncooked rice, or ceramic or metal pie weights. Bake the crust until set. Remove the foil and weights and either return the crust to the oven to finish baking or cool it completely.

BEATING EGG WHITES

• Eggs separate more easily when cold, but egg whites reach their fullest volume if allowed to stand at room temperature for 30 minutes before beating.

• When beating egg whites, always check that the bowl and beaters are completely clean and dry. The smallest trace of yolk, water or fat can prevent the whites from obtaining maximum volume. For best results, use a copper, stainless steel or glass bowl (plastic bowls may have an oily film, even after repeated washings).

• Beat the whites slowly until they are foamy, then increase the speed. Add a pinch of salt and cream of tartar at this point to help stabilize them. Do not overbeat or they will become dry and clump together.

• Beat the egg whites to the desired stage. For soft peaks, lift the beaters from the egg whites; they should form droopy, but definite, peaks. For stiff peaks, lift the beaters from the egg whites; stiff peaks should remain on the surface and the mixture will not slide around when the bowl is tilted.

• Immediately fold beaten egg whites gently into another mixture so volume is not lost; never beat or stir. To fold egg whites into another mixture, add egg whites and with a rubber spatula gently cut down to the bottom of the bowl. Then, scrape up side of bowl and fold over the top of the mixture. Repeat until the egg whites are fully incorporated.

DISSOLVING GELATIN

• To dissolve unflavored gelatin, sprinkle one envelope of gelatin over $1/4$ cup of cold liquid in a small saucepan. Let it stand for 3 minutes to soften. Stir over low heat about 5 minutes or until the gelatin is completely dissolved.

• Run a finger over the spoon to test for undissolved gelatin granules. If it feels granular, continue heating until it feels smooth.

WHIPPING CREAM

• For best results when beating whipping or heavy cream, first chill the cream, bowl and beaters—the cold keeps the fat in the cream solid, thus increasing the volume.

• For optimum volume, beat the cream in a deep, narrow bowl. Generally 1 cup of cream will yield 2 cups of whipped cream, so be sure to choose a bowl that will accommodate the increased volume. Beat the cream until soft peaks form. To test, lift the beaters from the whipping cream; the mixture should form droopy, but definite, peaks. Do not overbeat or the cream will form butter.

• For Sweetened Whipped Cream, beat cream until soft peaks form. Beat in 3 tablespoons sugar until stiff peaks form.

Mixed Berry Pie

**Traditional Double Pie
Crust (page 19)**
**2 cups canned or thawed
frozen blackberries,
well drained**
**1½ cups canned or thawed
frozen blueberries,
well drained**
**½ cup canned or thawed
frozen gooseberries,
well drained**
¼ cup sugar
3 tablespoons cornstarch
**⅛ teaspoon almond
extract**

1. Prepare pie crust following steps 1 and 2 of Traditional Double Pie Crust (page 19). Roll out and place bottom crust in pie plate following steps 3 through 6. Cover with plastic wrap and refrigerate 30 minutes to allow dough to relax.

2. Preheat oven to 425°F.

3. Combine blackberries, blueberries and gooseberries in large bowl. Add sugar, cornstarch and almond extract; stir well.

4. Spoon into prepared pie crust. Roll out top crust following steps 4 and 5 on page 18. Place top crust over filling following step 7 on page 19.

5. Trim edge leaving ½-inch overhang. Fold overhang under so crust is even with edge of pie plate. Press between thumb and forefinger to make stand-up edge. Cut slits in crust at ½-inch intervals around edge of pie to form flaps.

6. Press 1 flap in toward center of pie and the next out toward rim of pie plate. Continue alternating in and out around edge of pie.

7. Pierce top crust with fork to allow steam to escape.

8. Bake 40 minutes or until crust is golden brown. Cool completely on wire rack.

Makes 6 to 8 servings

My Golden Harvest Apple Pie

Traditional Double Pie
  Crust (page 19)
2 tablespoons all-purpose
  flour
2 pounds apples
½ cup sugar
1 teaspoon ground
  cinnamon
1 teaspoon ground
  nutmeg
3 tablespoons orange
  marmalade
2 tablespoons butter or
  margarine
Milk

1. Prepare pie crust following steps 1 and 2 of Traditional Double Pie Crust (page 19). Roll out and place bottom crust in pie plate following steps 3 through 6. Cover with plastic wrap and refrigerate 30 minutes to allow dough to relax. Sprinkle crust with flour.

2. Preheat oven to 450°F.

3. Peel apples. Remove cores; discard. Thinly slice apples.

4. Combine sugar, cinnamon and nutmeg in small bowl. Layer apple slices alternately with sugar mixture in pie crust.

5. Drop marmalade by teaspoonfuls on top of apples. Cut butter into 10 pieces. Place butter pieces on top of apples in pie crust.

6. Roll out top crust following steps 4 and 5 on page 18. Place top crust over filling following step 7 on page 19.

7. Trim edge leaving ½-inch overhang. Fold overhang under so crust is even with edge of pie plate.

8. To flute, place index finger on inside edge of rim, pointing toward outside of pie. Pinch crust into "V" shape between index finger and thumb of other hand. Repeat along edge.

9. Cut out designs in top crust with paring knife. Reroll dough scraps and cut out stem and leaf shapes. Brush top crust with milk. Place shapes on pie.

10. Bake 15 minutes. Reduce oven temperature to 375°F. Continue baking 30 to 35 minutes or until golden brown. Cool completely on wire rack.

Makes 6 to 8 servings

Praline Pumpkin Tart

1¼ cups all-purpose flour
1 tablespoon granulated sugar
¾ teaspoon salt, divided
¼ cup vegetable shortening
¼ cup butter or margarine
3 to 4 tablespoons cold water
1 can (16 ounces) pumpkin
1 can (13 ounces) evaporated milk (1½ cups)
2 eggs
⅔ cup packed brown sugar
1 teaspoon ground cinnamon
½ teaspoon ground ginger
¼ teaspoon ground cloves
Praline Topping (page 14)
Sweetened Whipped Cream (page 7)
Additional cinnamon and pecans halves for garnish

1. For crust, combine flour, granulated sugar and ¼ teaspoon salt in large bowl. Cut in shortening and butter using pastry blender or 2 knives until mixture forms pea-sized pieces.

2. Sprinkle flour mixture with water, 1 tablespoon at a time. Toss with fork until mixture holds together. Press together to form ball. Wrap in plastic wrap. Refrigerate about 1 hour or until chilled.

3. Remove plastic wrap from dough. Flatten dough into 5- to 6-inch disc. Lightly flour surface and rolling pin. Roll dough in short strokes starting in the middle of the disc rolling out toward the edge with rolling pin. Rotate dough ¼ turn to the right. Sprinkle more flour under dough and on rolling pin as necessary to prevent sticking. Continue to roll and rotate dough 2 to 3 more times. Roll out dough to ⅛-inch thickness.

4. Trim dough to 1 inch larger than inverted 10-inch tart pan with removable bottom or 1½ inches larger than inverted 9-inch pie plate. Place rolling pin on one side of dough. Gently roll dough over rolling pin once.

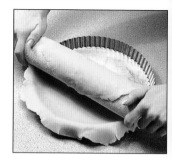

5. Carefully lift rolling pin and dough, unrolling dough over tart pan. Ease dough into tart pan with fingertips. Do not stretch dough. Cut dough even with edge of tart pan. (Roll and flute edge of dough in pie plate.)

6. Cover tart crust with plastic wrap and refrigerate 30 minutes to relax dough.

7. Preheat oven to 400°F.

continued on page 14

Praline Pumpkin Tart, continued

8. To blind bake tart crust, pierce tart crust with tines of fork at ¼-inch intervals, about 40 times.

9. Cut a square of foil about 4 inches larger than tart pan. Line tart pan with foil. Fill with dried beans, uncooked rice or ceramic pie weights.

10. Bake 10 minutes or until set. Remove from oven. Gently remove foil lining and beans. Return to oven and bake 5 minutes or until very light brown. Cool completely on wire rack. (If using beans or rice, save to use again for blind baking. The beans or rice are no longer usable in recipes.)

11. For filling, preheat oven to 400°F. Beat pumpkin, milk, eggs, brown sugar, 1 teaspoon cinnamon, remaining ½ teaspoon salt, ginger and cloves in large bowl with electric mixer at low speed. Pour into cooled tart crust. Bake 35 minutes.

12. Prepare Praline Topping. Sprinkle topping over center of tart leaving 1½-inch rim around edge of tart.

13. Bake 15 minutes more or until knife inserted 1 inch from center comes out clean.

14. Cool completely on wire rack. Prepare Sweetened Whipped Cream and spoon into decorating bag with fluted tip. Pipe whipped cream around edge of pie, making decorative edge. Sprinkle additional cinnamon over whipped cream. Garnish with pecan halves.

Makes 8 servings

Praline Topping

- ⅓ **cup packed brown sugar**
- ⅓ **cup chopped pecans**
- ⅓ **cup uncooked quick-cooking oats**
- 1 **tablespoon butter or margarine, softened**

Place sugar, pecans and oats in small bowl. Cut in butter with pastry blender or 2 knives until crumbs form.

Chocolate Hazelnut Pie

Chocolate Hazelnut Crust (page 16)
1 envelope unflavored gelatin
¼ cup cold water
2 cups whipping cream, divided
1½ cups semisweet chocolate chips
2 eggs*
3 tablespoons hazelnut-flavored liqueur
1 teaspoon vanilla
24 caramels, unwrapped
Caramel Flowers for garnish (page 16)

Use clean, uncracked eggs.

1. Prepare Chocolate Hazelnut Crust; set aside.

2. Sprinkle gelatin over water in small saucepan. Let stand without stirring 3 minutes for gelatin to soften. Heat over low heat, stirring constantly, until gelatin is completely dissolved, about 5 minutes. To test for undissolved gelatin, run a finger over the spoon. If it is smooth, the gelatin is completely dissolved; if it feels granular, continue heating until it feels smooth.

3. Stir 1 cup whipping cream into gelatin mixture. Heat just to a boil; remove from heat. Add chocolate chips. Stir until chocolate is melted.

4. Add eggs; beat well. Add ½ cup whipping cream, liqueur and vanilla; beat well. Pour into large bowl; refrigerate about 15 minutes or until thickened.

5. Combine caramels and remaining ½ cup whipping cream in small saucepan. Simmer over low heat, stirring occasionally, until completely melted and smooth.

6. Pour caramel mixture into prepared crust; let stand about 10 minutes.

7. Beat thickened gelatin mixture with electric mixer at medium speed until smooth. Pour over caramel layer; refrigerate 3 hours or until firm. Garnish, if desired.

Makes 6 to 8 servings

continued on page 16

*Chocolate Hazelnut Pie,
continued*

Chocolate Hazelnut Crust

¾ **cup hazelnuts**
30 chocolate cookie wafers
½ **cup melted butter or
 margarine**

1. Preheat oven to 350°F.

2. To toast hazelnuts, spread hazelnuts in single layer on baking sheet. Bake 10 to 12 minutes or until toasted and skins begin to flake off; let cool slightly. Wrap hazelnuts in heavy kitchen towel; rub towel back and forth to remove as much of the skins as possible.

3. Combine cookies and hazelnuts in food processor or blender container; process with on/off pulses until finely crushed.

4. Combine cookie crumb mixture and butter in medium bowl. Press firmly onto bottom and up side of 9-inch pie plate, forming a high rim.

5. Bake 10 minutes; cool completely on wire rack.

Caramel Flowers
6 to 8 caramels

1. Place 1 fresh, soft caramel between 2 sheets of waxed paper.

2. With rolling pin, roll out caramel to 2-inch oval (press down hard with rolling pin).

3. Starting at 1 corner, roll caramel into a cone to resemble a flower. Repeat with remaining caramels. Before serving, place 1 Caramel Flower on each piece of pie.

Traditional Single Pie Crust

1⅓ cups all-purpose flour
½ teaspoon salt
½ cup shortening
3 tablespoons cold water

1. Combine flour and salt in large bowl. Cut in shortening using pastry blender or 2 knives until mixture forms pea-sized pieces.

2. Sprinkle with water, 1 tablespoon at a time. Toss with fork until mixture holds together. Press together to form a ball.

3. Press dough between hands to form 5- to 6-inch disk.

4. Lightly flour work surface and rolling pin. Roll dough in short strokes, starting in middle of disk and rolling out toward edge. Rotate dough ¼ turn to right. Sprinkle more flour under dough and on rolling pin as necessary to prevent sticking. Continue to roll and rotate dough 2 to 3 more times.

5. Roll dough into ⅛-inch-thick circle at least 1 inch larger than inverted pie plate.

6. Place rolling pin on 1 side of dough. Gently roll dough over rolling pin once.

7. Carefully lift rolling pin and dough. Unroll dough over pie plate. Ease dough into pie plate with fingertips. Do not stretch dough.

8. Trim crust, leaving ½-inch overhang. Fold overhang under. Flute as desired. Cover pie crust with plastic wrap and refrigerate 30 minutes to allow dough to relax.

Traditional Double Pie Crust

2 cups all-purpose flour
1 teaspoon salt
¾ cup shortening
5 tablespoons cold water

1. Combine flour and salt in large bowl. Cut in shortening using pastry blender or 2 knives until mixture forms pea-sized pieces.

2. Sprinkle with water, 1 tablespoon at a time. Toss with fork until mixture holds together. Press together to form a ball.

3. Divide dough in half. Press each half between hands to form 5- to 6-inch disk.

4. Roll out each half as described in Classic Single Pie Crust, steps 4 and 5.

5. Place rolling pin on 1 side of dough. Gently roll dough over rolling pin once. Carefully lift rolling pin and dough.

6. Unroll dough over pie plate. Ease dough into pie plate with fingertips. Do not stretch dough. Trim edge even with edge of pie crust. Cover pie crust with plastic wrap and refrigerate 30 minutes to allow dough to relax.

7. Add desired filling to unbaked pie crust. Moisten edge of crust with water. Lift top crust onto filled pie as described in step 5. Unroll over filling. Pierce top crust with fork to allow steam to escape.

8. Trim crust leaving ½-inch overhang. Fold overhang under bottom crust. Flute as desired.

Mini Chocolate Chip Cake

2 cups all-purpose flour
1 cup packed dark brown
    sugar
1 tablespoon baking
    powder
1 teaspoon salt
½ teaspoon baking soda
½ cup granulated sugar
½ cup shortening
3 eggs
1¼ cups milk
1½ teaspoons vanilla
½ cup semisweet
    chocolate chips, finely
    chopped
    Butterscotch Filling
    (page 22)
    Chocolate Chip Glaze
    (page 22)
½ cup finely chopped
    walnuts, divided
    Fresh raspberries and
    mint leaves for
    garnish

1. Preheat oven to 350°F.

2. Grease bottom and sides of two 9-inch round baking pans. Add 2 to 3 teaspoons flour to each pan. Gently tap side of pan to evenly coat bottom and sides with flour.

3. Combine flour, brown sugar, baking powder, salt and baking soda in small bowl. Set aside.

4. Beat granulated sugar and shortening in large bowl with electric mixer at medium speed until light and fluffy, scraping down side of bowl once.

5. Add eggs, 1 at a time, beating well after each addition.

6. Add milk and vanilla; beat at low speed until well blended. Add flour mixture and chocolate chips. Beat at low speed until blended. Beat at medium speed until smooth, scraping bowl occasionally. Pour into prepared pans.

7. Bake 40 to 45 minutes or until cake tester or wooden pick inserted into center comes out clean. Cool 15 minutes. Remove from pan to wire rack; cool completely.

continued on page 22

Mini Chocolate Chip Cake, continued

8. Prepare Butterscotch Filling and Chocolate Chip Glaze.

9. Place 1 cake layer on serving plate. Spread with Butterscotch Filling; sprinkle with ¼ cup walnuts. Top with second cake layer.

10. Pour Chocolate Chip Glaze over top of cake, allowing some of glaze to drip down side of cake. Sprinkle remaining ¼ cup walnuts on top. Garnish, if desired.

Makes 8 to 10 servings

Butterscotch Filling

½ cup packed light brown
  sugar
2 tablespoons cornstarch
¼ teaspoon salt
½ cup water
1 tablespoon butter

1. Combine brown sugar, cornstarch and salt in medium saucepan. Add water; cook over medium heat until mixture comes to a boil, stirring constantly. Boil 1 minute until mixture thickens, stirring constantly.

2. Add butter; stir until melted. Cool completely.

Chocolate Chip Glaze

½ cup semisweet
  chocolate chips
2 tablespoons butter
1 tablespoon light corn
  syrup

Combine chocolate chips, butter and corn syrup in small saucepan. Cook over low heat until chocolate melts, stirring constantly. Cool slightly.

Sour Cream Pound Cake

1 orange
1 cup butter, softened
2¾ cups sugar
1 tablespoon vanilla
6 eggs
3 cups all-purpose flour
½ teaspoon salt
¼ teaspoon baking soda
1 cup sour cream
Citrus Topping (page 24)

1. Preheat oven to 325°F. Grease 10-inch tube pan.

2. Finely grate colored portion of orange peel using bell grater or hand-held grater. Measure 2 teaspoons orange peel; set aside.

3. Beat butter in large bowl at medium speed of electric mixer until creamy, scraping down side of bowl once. Gradually add sugar, beating until light and fluffy. Beat in vanilla and orange peel.

4. Add eggs, 1 at a time, beating 1 minute after each addition.

5. Combine flour, salt and baking soda in small bowl. Add to butter mixture alternately with sour cream, beginning and ending with flour mixture. Beat well after each addition. Pour into prepared pan.

6. Bake 1 hour and 15 minutes or until cake tester or wooden skewer inserted in center comes out clean.

7. Prepare Citrus Topping. Spoon over hot cake; cool in pan 15 minutes. Remove from pan to wire rack, topping side up; cool completely.

Makes 10 to 12 servings

continued on page 24

Sour Cream Pound Cake,
continued

Citrus Topping

2 oranges
2 teaspoons salt
½ cup sugar, divided
⅓ cup lemon juice
1 teaspoon vanilla

1. With citrus zester or vegetable peeler, remove colored peel, not white pith, from oranges. Measure ⅓ cup.

2. To juice oranges, cut oranges in half on cutting board.

3. Using citrus reamer, squeeze juice from oranges into measuring cup or small bowl. Measure ⅓ cup.

4. Combine orange peel and salt in medium saucepan. Add enough water to cover.

5. Bring to a boil over high heat. Boil 2 minutes. Drain in fine-meshed sieve. Return orange peel to saucepan.

6. Add orange juice and ¼ cup sugar to saucepan. Bring to a boil over high heat. Reduce heat; simmer 10 minutes. Remove from heat.

7. Add remaining ¼ cup sugar, lemon juice and vanilla; stir until smooth.

Carrot Cake

¾ **pound carrots**
4 **eggs**
1¼ **cups vegetable oil**
2 **cups all-purpose flour**
1½ **cups sugar**
2 **teaspoons baking
   powder**
1 **teaspoon baking soda**
2 **teaspoons ground
   cinnamon**
¼ **teaspoon salt**
1 **cup coarsely chopped
   pecans or walnuts
   Cream Cheese Icing
   (recipe follows)**

1. Trim ends of carrots; discard. Peel carrots. Shred with shredding disk of food processor or hand shredder. Measure 2½ cups; set aside.

2. Preheat oven to 350°F. Grease and flour sides of 13×9-inch baking pan. (Technique on page 20.)

3. Beat eggs and oil in small bowl. Combine flour, sugar, baking powder, baking soda, cinnamon and salt in large bowl. Add egg mixture; mix well. Stir in carrots and pecans. Pour into prepared pan.

4. Bake 40 to 45 minutes or until cake tester or wooden pick inserted in center comes out clean. Cool completely on wire rack.

5. Prepare Cream Cheese Icing. Spread over cooled cake. Garnish, if desired.

Makes 8 to 10 servings

Cream Cheese Icing
4 **cups (16-ounce box)
   powdered sugar**
1 **package (8 ounces)
   cream cheese,
   softened**
½ **cup margarine, softened**
1 **teaspoon vanilla**

1. Sift powdered sugar into large bowl with fine-meshed sieve or sifter.

2. Beat cream cheese, margarine and vanilla in another large bowl with electric mixer at medium speed until smooth, scraping down side of bowl occasionally.

3. Gradually add powdered sugar. Beat with electric mixer at low speed until well blended, scraping down side of bowl occasionally.

Makes about 1½ cups

Apricot Meringue Squares

1 orange
1 cup butter, softened
⅓ cup granulated sugar
1 teaspoon vanilla
2 cups all-purpose flour
1 jar (12 ounces) apricot jam
2 egg whites (technique on page 38)
1 cup powdered sugar
Slivered almonds for garnish

1. Finely grate colored portion of orange peel using bell grater or hand-held grater. Measure 2 teaspoons orange peel; set aside.

2. To juice orange, cut orange in half on cutting board. Using citrus reamer, squeeze juice from orange into measuring cup or small bowl. (Technique on page 24.) Measure 2 tablespoons juice; set aside.

3. Preheat oven to 350°F.

4. Beat butter, granulated sugar, vanilla and orange peel in large bowl with electric mixer at medium speed until light and fluffy, scraping down side of bowl once. Gradually add flour, beating at low speed until smooth.

5. Press into ungreased 13×9-inch baking pan. Bake 15 minutes. Cool completely on wire rack.

6. Combine jam and orange juice in small bowl; beat until smooth. Spread over cooled crust.

7. To make meringue, beat egg whites in clean large bowl with electric mixer at high speed until foamy. Gradually beat in powdered sugar until stiff peaks form. After beaters are lifted from meringue, stiff peaks should remain on surface, and mixture will not slide around when bowl is tilted. (Technique on page 44.)

8. Spread meringue over jam mixture with rubber spatula.

9. Bake at 350°F 15 to 20 minutes or until light golden brown. Cool completely on wire rack. Cut into 2-inch squares. Garnish, if desired.

Makes about 2 dozen squares

Walnut Fudge

4 cups sugar
½ cup margarine
1 can (12 ounces) evaporated milk
3 tablespoons light corn syrup
1 pound white chocolate chips*
1 jar (13 ounces) marshmallow creme
1 cup chopped walnuts
1 tablespoon vanilla

*Do not use compound chocolate or confectioner's coating.

1. Line 13×9-inch pan with foil, leaving 1-inch over-hang on sides to use for handles when lifting fudge out of pan. Lightly butter foil.

2. Combine sugar, margarine, evaporated milk and corn syrup in large saucepan; stir well. Bring to a boil over medium heat, stirring only until sugar dissolves.

3. Attach candy thermometer to side of pan, making sure bulb is completely submerged in sugar mixture but not touching bottom of pan.

4. Continue heating, without stirring, until mixture reaches soft-ball stage (234°F) on candy thermometer.

5. Remove from heat and add white chocolate chips. Stir with wooden spoon until melted. Add marshmallow creme, walnuts and vanilla, stirring well after each addition.

6. Pour into prepared pan. Score into squares by cutting halfway through fudge with sharp knife while fudge is still warm.

7. Remove from pan by lifting fudge and foil using foil handles. Place on cutting board. Cool completely. Cut along score lines into squares. Remove foil.

Makes about 3 pounds

Chocolate Chiffon Cake

1 cup all-purpose flour
1 teaspoon baking
   powder
½ teaspoon salt
1 bar (4 ounces)
   German's sweet
   baking chocolate
½ cup hot water
5 eggs, separated
   (technique on page
   38)
⅔ cup granulated sugar
1 teaspoon vanilla
   Powdered sugar

1. Preheat oven to 350°F.

2. Combine flour, baking powder and salt in small bowl; set aside.

3. Combine chocolate and hot water in small, heavy saucepan. Melt chocolate over low heat, stirring occasionally; set aside.

4. Beat egg whites in clean large bowl with electric mixer at high speed until foamy. Gradually beat in sugar until stiff peaks form; set aside.

5. Combine melted chocolate mixture, egg yolks and vanilla in large bowl. Beat with electric mixer at low speed until well blended, scraping down side of bowl once.

6. Gradually add flour mixture to chocolate mixture. Beat with electric mixer at low speed until well blended.

7. Fold chocolate mixture into egg white mixture.

8. Pour into ungreased 10-inch tube pan. Run long metal spatula through batter to break up any large air bubbles.

9. Bake 45 to 50 minutes or until top springs back when lightly touched with finger.

10. Invert cake in pan onto heatproof bottle or funnel. Cool completely.

11. Remove from pan. Sift powdered sugar through fine-meshed sieve or sifter onto top of cake.

Makes about 12 servings

Orange Cappuccino Brownies

¾ **cup butter**
2 **squares (1 ounce each)**
    semisweet chocolate,
    coarsely chopped
2 **squares (1 ounce each)**
    unsweetened
    chocolate, coarsely
    chopped
1¾ **cups granulated sugar**
1 **tablespoon instant**
    espresso powder or
    instant coffee
    granules
3 **eggs**
¼ **cup orange-flavored**
    liqueur
2 **teaspoons grated**
    orange peel
    (technique on page
    28)
1 **cup all-purpose flour**
1 **package (12 ounces)**
    semisweet chocolate
    chips
2 **tablespoons shortening**
1 **orange for garnish**

1. Preheat oven to 350°F. Grease 13×9-inch baking pan.

2. Melt butter, chopped semisweet chocolate and unsweetened chocolate in large heavy saucepan over low heat, stirring constantly. Stir in granulated sugar and espresso powder. Remove from heat. Cool slightly.

3. Beat in eggs, 1 at a time, with wire whisk. Whisk in liqueur and orange peel.

4. Beat flour into chocolate mixture until just blended. Spread batter evenly into prepared baking pan.

5. Bake 25 to 30 minutes or until center is just set. Remove pan to wire rack.

6. Meanwhile, melt chocolate chips and shortening in small, heavy saucepan over low heat, stirring constantly.

7. Immediately after removing brownies from oven, spread hot chocolate mixture over warm brownies. Cool completely in pan on wire rack. Cut into 2-inch squares.

8. To make orange peel garnish, remove thin strips of peel from orange using citrus stripper.

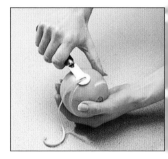

9. Tie strips into knots or twist into spirals. Garnish, if desired.

Makes about 2 dozen brownies

Raspberry Chocolate Mousse Pie

40 chocolate wafer cookies
¼ cup butter, melted
6 squares (1 ounce each) semisweet chocolate
1¼ cups whipping cream
½ cup water
7 tablespoons sugar
5 egg yolks (technique on page 38)
3 tablespoons raspberry-flavored liqueur
Sweetened Whipped Cream (page 7), fresh raspberries and mint leaves for garnish

1. Place cookies in food processor or blender container; process with on/off pulses until finely crushed.

2. Combine cookie crumbs and butter in medium bowl; mix well. Press firmly onto bottom and 1 inch up side of 9-inch springform pan.

3. Melt chocolate in top of double boiler over hot, not boiling, water. Cool slightly.

4. Beat whipping cream with electric mixer at high speed until soft peaks form. (Technique on page 40.) Refrigerate.

5. Combine water and sugar in small saucepan. Bring to a boil over medium-high heat. Boil 1 minute. Place hot syrup in 1-cup glass measure.

6. Place egg yolks in large, deep, heatproof bowl. Whisk in hot syrup. Place bowl in large saucepan of hot, not boiling, water. Continue to whisk until soft peaks form. To test, lift whisk; mixture should form droopy, but definite, peaks. Remove from heat.

7. Beat mixture until cool. Stir in melted chocolate and liqueur.

8. Stir ½ cup whipped cream into chocolate mixture.

9. Fold in remaining whipped cream. (Technique on page 40.)

10. Pour into prepared crust. Refrigerate until firm, about 3 hours or overnight.

11. To serve, remove side of pan. Garnish, if desired.

Makes 10 servings

Almond Chocolate Crown

2 packages (3 ounces
    each) ladyfingers
4 eggs*
1 cup milk
1 envelope unflavored
    gelatin
1 cup sugar, divided
⅔ cup unsweetened cocoa
    powder
¼ cup almond-flavored
    liqueur
1½ cups whipping cream
    Almond Cream (page
    40)
    Sliced almonds for
    garnish

*Use clean, uncracked eggs.

1. Gently split ladyfingers using serrated knife. Line bottom and side of 9-inch springform pan with split ladyfingers, cut side facing in. Refrigerate.

2. To separate egg yolk from white, gently tap egg in center against hard surface, such as side of bowl. Holding shell half in each hand, gently transfer yolk back and forth between the 2 shell halves. Allow white to drip down between the 2 halves into bowl.

3. When all the white has dripped into bowl, place yolk in another bowl. Transfer white to third bowl. Repeat with remaining 3 eggs. (Egg whites must be free from any egg yolk to reach the proper volume when beaten.)

4. Combine egg yolks and milk in small bowl; beat well.

5. Combine gelatin, ¾ cup sugar and cocoa in medium saucepan.

6. Add egg yolk mixture to gelatin mixture. Let stand, without stirring, 3 minutes for gelatin to soften.

7. Heat over low heat, stirring constantly, until gelatin is completely dissolved, about 5 minutes. To test for undissolved gelatin, run a finger over the spoon. If it is smooth, the gelatin is completely dissolved; if it feels granular, continue heating until it feels smooth.

8. Remove from heat. Using wire whisk, beat until completely blended. Whisk in liqueur.

9. Pour mixture into large bowl. Place bowl in refrigerator; stir mixture occasionally. Chill until mixture mounds slightly when dropped from spoon. (Technique on page 41.) Remove from refrigerator.

continued on page 40

Almond Chocolate Crown, continued

10. Chill large bowl and beaters thoroughly. Pour chilled whipping cream into chilled bowl and beat with electric mixer at high speed until soft peaks form. To test, lift beaters from whipping cream; mixture should form droopy, but definite, peaks. Refrigerate.

11. Clean beaters thoroughly. Beat egg whites in separate clean large bowl with electric mixer at high speed until foamy. Gradually beat in remaining ¼ cup sugar until stiff peaks form; set aside.

12. Fold gelatin mixture into egg white mixture with rubber spatula by gently cutting down to bottom of bowl, scraping up side of bowl, then folding over top of mixture. Repeat until gelatin mixture is evenly incorporated into egg white mixture.

13. Fold whipped cream into egg white mixture as described in step 12. Pour mixture into ladyfinger-lined pan. Refrigerate 4 hours or overnight until firm.

14. Prepare Almond Cream. To serve, remove side of pan. Cut into serving pieces. Serve with Almond Cream. Garnish, if desired.

Makes about 12 servings

Almond Cream
½ cup whipping cream
1 tablespoon powdered sugar
1 tablespoon almond-flavored liqueur

1. Chill small bowl and beaters thoroughly. Pour chilled whipping cream into chilled bowl and beat with electric mixer at high speed until thickened. Add powdered sugar and beat until soft peaks form. To test, lift beaters from whipping cream; mixture should form droopy, but definite, peaks.

2. Fold in almond-flavored liqueur as described in step 12 of main recipe.

Makes about 1 cup

Black Forest Soufflé

3 eggs*
2 cups milk
2 envelopes unflavored
    gelatin
¾ cup sugar, divided
4 squares (1 ounce each)
    semisweet chocolate,
    chopped
2 teaspoons rum extract
1½ teaspoons vanilla
2 cups whipping cream,
    divided
1 can (21 ounces) cherry
    pie filling
⅓ cup chopped almonds
    Chocolate Curls (page
    42) for garnish
    Maraschino cherries for
    garnish

*Use clean, uncracked eggs.

1. Cut 18×16-inch piece of waxed paper. Fold lengthwise in half. Grease and flour. Wrap waxed paper around rim of 1½-quart soufflé dish, greased side in, forming a "collar." Waxed paper should extend at least 4 inches above rim of soufflé dish. Tape to secure in place.

2. Separate egg yolks from whites. (Technique on page 38.)

3. Combine egg yolks and milk in small bowl; beat until well combined.

4. Combine gelatin and ½ cup sugar in medium saucepan. Add egg yolk mixture to gelatin mixture. Let stand, without stirring, 3 minutes for gelatin to soften.

5. Heat over low heat, stirring constantly, until gelatin is completely dissolved, about 5 minutes. To test for undissolved gelatin, run a finger over the spoon. If it is smooth, the gelatin is completely dissolved; if it feels granular, continue heating until it feels smooth.

6. Add chopped chocolate to dissolved gelatin mixture; stir until completely melted. Beat with wire whisk until thoroughly blended. Stir in rum extract and vanilla.

7. Pour mixture into large bowl. Place bowl in refrigerator; stir mixture occasionally. Chill until mixture mounds slightly when dropped from spoon. Remove from refrigerator.

8. To make meringue, beat egg whites in clean large bowl with electric mixer at high speed until foamy. Gradually beat in remaining ¼ cup sugar until stiff peaks form. After beaters are lifted from meringue, stiff peaks should remain on surface, and mixture will not slide around when bowl is tilted. (Technique on page 44.)

continued on page 42

Black Forest Soufflé, continued

9. Fold meringue into chocolate-gelatin mixture with rubber spatula by gently cutting down to bottom of bowl, scraping up side of bowl, then folding over top of mixture. Repeat until egg whites are evenly incorporated into chocolate-gelatin mixture.

10. Chill large bowl and beaters thoroughly. Pour chilled whipping cream into chilled bowl and beat with electric mixer at high speed until soft peaks form. To test, lift beaters from whipping cream; mixture should form droopy, but definite, peaks.

11. Fold 3 cups whipped cream into chocolate-gelatin mixture as described in step 9. Reserve remaining whipped cream for garnish.

12. Fold cherry pie filling and almonds into chocolate mixture as described in step 9.

13. Pour mixture into prepared dish; refrigerate until set.

14. Prepare Chocolate Curls. To serve, remove collar. Garnish, if desired.

Makes about 10 servings

Chocolate Curls
2 squares (1 ounce each) semisweet chocolate

1. Allow chocolate to soften by setting in warm place for 30 minutes. Chocolate should still be firm.

2. Make chocolate curls using vegetable peeler.

3. Carefully pick up each chocolate curl by inserting a wooden toothpick in center. Lift to waxed paper-lined baking sheet. Refrigerate about 15 minutes until firm.

Double Chocolate Bombe

5 eggs, divided*
1½ cups whipping cream,
    divided
1 envelope unflavored
    gelatin
1 package (12 ounces)
    semisweet chocolate
    chips
¼ teaspoon salt
⅓ cup sugar
    Chocolate Cake (page
    46)
    White Chocolate
    Cutouts (page 47) for
    garnish
1 white chocolate baking
    bar (2 ounces) for
    drizzling

*Use clean, uncracked eggs.

1. Line 2-quart bowl with plastic wrap; oil lightly.

2. To separate egg white from yolk, gently tap egg in center against hard surface, such as side of bowl. Holding shell half in each hand, gently transfer yolk back and forth between the 2 shell halves. Allow white to drip down between the 2 halves into bowl.

3. When all white has dripped into bowl, place yolk in another bowl. Transfer white to third bowl. Repeat with remaining 4 eggs. (Egg whites must be free from any egg yolk to reach the proper volume when beaten.)

4. Place egg yolks and ½ cup whipping cream in small bowl; beat slightly with fork. Sprinkle gelatin over egg yolk mixture. Let stand without stirring 5 minutes to soften.

5. Melt chocolate chips in top of double boiler over hot, not boiling, water.

6. Stir about ½ cup melted chocolate into egg yolk mixture.

7. Stir egg yolk mixture back into remaining chocolate in top of double boiler. Continue to heat until gelatin is completely dissolved

8. To make meringue, beat egg whites and salt in clean large bowl with electric mixer at high speed until foamy. Gradually beat in sugar until stiff peaks form. After beaters are lifted from meringue, stiff peaks should remain on surface, and mixture will not slide around when bowl is tilted.

continued on page 46

Double Chocolate Bombe, continued

9. Fold in chocolate mixture with rubber spatula by gently cutting down to bottom of bowl, scraping up side of bowl, then folding over top of mixture. Repeat until chocolate mixture is evenly incorporated into meringue.

10. Beat remaining 1 cup whipping cream until soft peaks form. (Technique on page 40.)

11. Fold into chocolate mixture as described in step 9.

12. Pour into prepared bowl. Cover and refrigerate at least 4 hours.

13. Prepare Chocolate Cake and White Chocolate Cutouts.

14. Place cake on serving plate. Unmold mousse onto cake. Remove plastic wrap. Trim edge of cake around mousse, if desired.

15. Place white chocolate baking bar in small resealable plastic freezer bag. Microwave at MEDIUM (50% power) 2 minutes. Turn bag over; microwave at MEDIUM (50% power) 2 to 3 minutes or until chocolate is melted. Knead bag until chocolate is smooth.

16. Cut off very tiny corner of bag; drizzle white chocolate over mousse. Refrigerate until white chocolate is set, about 30 minutes. Garnish with White Chocolate Cutouts, if desired.

Makes about 8 servings

Chocolate Cake

- 1 cup sugar
- ⅓ cup shortening
- 2 eggs
- ⅓ cup water
- ½ teaspoon vanilla
- 1 cup all-purpose flour
- ⅓ cup unsweetened cocoa powder
- 1 teaspoon baking soda
- ¼ teaspoon baking powder
- ¼ teaspoon salt

1. Preheat oven to 375°F. Grease bottom and side of 9-inch round baking pan. Add 2 to 3 teaspoons flour to pan. Gently tap side of pan to evenly coat bottom and side with flour.

$2.$ Combine sugar and shortening in large bowl. Beat with electric mixer at medium speed until light and fluffy, scraping down side of bowl once. Add eggs, water and vanilla; beat well.

$3.$ Combine flour, cocoa, baking soda, baking powder and salt in small bowl. Add to shortening mixture; beat with electric mixer at medium speed until smooth. Pour batter into prepared pan.

$4.$ Bake 20 to 25 minutes or until cake tester or wooden pick inserted into center comes out clean. Cool 10 minutes in pan.

$5.$ Loosen edge and remove to wire rack; cool completely.

White Chocolate Cutouts
2 white chocolate baking bars (2 ounces each), coarsely chopped

$1.$ Melt chocolate in small bowl set in bowl of very hot water, stirring occasionally. This will take about 10 minutes.

$2.$ Spread onto waxed paper-lined cookie sheet. Refrigerate until firm, about 15 minutes.

$3.$ Cut into large triangle shapes with sharp knife.

$4.$ Immediately lift shapes carefully from waxed paper with spatula or knife. Refrigerate until ready to use.

Apples 'n' Honey Nut Tart

1¼ cups all-purpose flour
⅓ cup wheat germ
⅓ cup packed brown
sugar
½ teaspoon salt
¾ teaspoon grated orange
peel, divided
(technique on page
28)
½ cup cold butter, cut into
pieces
1 egg, beaten
1 cup coarsely chopped
pecans
⅓ cup golden raisins
2½ pounds apples
8 tablespoons honey,
divided
2 tablespoons butter,
melted
½ teaspoon ground
cinnamon
⅓ cup orange marmalade
⅔ cup whipping cream

1. Combine flour, wheat germ, brown sugar, salt and ½ teaspoon grated orange peel in large bowl. Cut in cold butter with pastry blender or 2 knives until mixture forms pea-sized pieces. Add egg; stir until well blended.

2. Press firmly onto bottom and up side of 9-inch tart pan with removable bottom. Freeze until very firm, about 30 minutes.

3. Preheat oven to 350°F.

4. Combine pecans and raisins in small bowl. Sprinkle on bottom of chilled crust.

5. Peel apples. For center slice, place peeled apple, with stem facing away from you, on cutting board. Cut a ¼-inch-thick slice from center of apple. Place in center of tart.

6. Remove cores from remaining apples; discard. Cut apples into ¼-inch-thick slices.

7. Combine 6 tablespoons honey, melted butter, remaining ¼ teaspoon orange peel, cinnamon and apple slices in large bowl; stir to coat apples.

8. Arrange apple slices in circular pattern on top of pecans and raisins around center apple slice. Drizzle any honey mixture left in bowl over apples. Bake 50 to 55 minutes or until apples are tender.

9. Place marmalade in small saucepan. Heat over medium heat until warm, stirring occasionally. Brush over apples. Cool; remove side of tart pan.

10. Beat whipping cream and remaining 2 tablespoons honey until soft peaks form. (Technique on page 40.) Serve tart with whipped cream.

Makes 8 to 10 servings.

Spiced Pear Tart

30 gingersnap cookies
½ cup chopped pecans
⅓ cup butter, melted
1 cup sour cream
¾ cup half-and-half
1 package (4-serving size)
    vanilla instant
    pudding mix
2 tablespoons apricot
    brandy
4 ripe pears*
⅓ cup packed dark brown
    sugar
½ teaspoon ground ginger

*Or, substitute 1 (16-ounce) can pear halves, drained and thinly sliced, for fresh pears.

1. Preheat oven to 350°F.

2. Combine cookies and pecans in food processor or blender container; process with on/off pulses until finely crushed.

3. Combine crumb mixture and butter in medium bowl. Press firmly onto bottom and up side of 10-inch quiche dish or 9-inch pie plate. Bake 7 minutes; cool completely on wire rack.

4. Combine sour cream and half-and-half in large bowl. Beat until smooth. Whisk in pudding mix. Add apricot brandy. Beat until smooth.

5. Pour into prepared crust. Cover; refrigerate several hours or overnight.

6. Just before serving, preheat broiler. Peel pears with vegetable peeler. Cut pears in half lengthwise. Remove cores and seeds; discard. Cut pears into thin slices.

7. Arrange pear slices in overlapping circles on top of pudding mixture.

8. Combine brown sugar and ginger in small bowl. Sprinkle evenly over pears. Broil 4 to 6 minutes or until sugar is melted and bubbly. Watch carefully so sugar does not burn. Serve immediately.

Makes 6 to 8 servings

Crunchy Peach Cobbler

1 can (29 ounces) or
   2 cans (16 ounces
   each) cling peach
   slices in syrup
⅓ cup plus 1 tablespoon
   granulated sugar,
   divided
1 tablespoon cornstarch
½ teaspoon vanilla
½ cup packed brown
   sugar
2 cups all-purpose flour,
   divided
⅓ cup uncooked rolled
   oats
¼ cup margarine or butter,
   melted
½ teaspoon ground
   cinnamon
½ teaspoon salt
½ cup shortening
4 to 5 tablespoons cold
   water
   Sweetened Whipped
   Cream (page 7) for
   garnish

1. Drain peach slices in fine-meshed sieve over 2-cup glass measure. Reserve ¾ cup syrup.

2. Combine ⅓ cup granulated sugar and cornstarch in small saucepan. Slowly add reserved syrup. Stir well. Add vanilla. Cook over low heat, stirring constantly, until thickened. Set aside.

3. Combine brown sugar, ½ cup flour, oats, margarine and cinnamon in small bowl; stir until mixture forms coarse crumbs. Set aside.

4. Preheat oven to 350°F.

5. Combine remaining 1½ cups flour, 1 tablespoon granulated sugar and salt in small bowl. Cut in shortening with pastry blender or 2 knives until mixture forms pea-sized pieces.

6. Sprinkle water, 1 tablespoon at a time, over flour mixture. Toss lightly with fork until mixture holds together. Press together to form a ball.

7. Roll out dough into square ⅛ inch thick, following steps 3 and 4 on page 18. Cut into 10-inch square.

8. Fold dough in half, then in half again. Carefully place folded dough in center of 8×8-inch baking dish. Unfold and press onto bottom and about 1 inch up sides of dish.

9. Arrange peaches over crust. Pour sauce over peaches. Sprinkle with crumb topping.

10. Bake 45 minutes. Prepare Sweetened Whipped Cream. Serve warm or at room temperature with Sweetened Whipped Cream.

Makes about 6 servings

Raspberry Cheesecake Blossoms

3 packages (10 ounces each) frozen raspberries, thawed
¼ cup butter, melted
8 sheets phyllo dough*
1 package (8 ounces) cream cheese, softened
½ cup cottage cheese
1 egg
½ cup plus 3 tablespoons sugar, divided
4 teaspoons lemon juice, divided
½ teaspoon vanilla
Fresh raspberries and sliced kiwifruit for garnish

*Cover with plastic wrap, then a damp kitchen towel to prevent dough from drying out.

1. Drain thawed raspberries in fine-meshed sieve over 1-cup glass measure. Reserve syrup.

2. Preheat oven to 350°F. Grease 12 (2½-inch) muffin cups.

3. Brush melted butter onto 1 phyllo sheet. Cover with second phyllo sheet; brush with butter. Repeat with remaining sheets of phyllo.

4. Cut stack of phyllo dough in half lengthwise and then in thirds crosswise, to make a total of 12 squares. Gently fit each stacked square into prepared muffin cup.

5. Place cream cheese, cottage cheese, egg, 3 tablespoons sugar, 1 teaspoon lemon juice and vanilla in food processor or blender. Process until smooth. Divide mixture evenly among muffin cups.

6. Bake 10 to 15 minutes or until lightly browned. Carefully remove from muffin cups to wire racks to cool.

7. Bring reserved raspberry syrup to a boil in small saucepan over medium-high heat. Cook until reduced to ¾ cup, stirring occasionally.

8. Place thawed raspberries in food processor or blender. Process until smooth. Press through fine-meshed sieve with back of spoon to remove seeds.

9. Combine raspberry puree, reduced syrup, remaining ½ cup sugar and 3 teaspoons lemon juice in small bowl. Mix well.

10. To serve, spoon raspberry sauce onto 12 dessert plates. Place cheesecake blossom on each plate. Garnish, if desired.

Makes 12 servings

Maple Sweetheart

**1 package (3 ounces)
ladyfingers, split
2 tablespoons unflavored
gelatin
¼ cup cold water
½ cup real maple syrup
5 eggs*
2 cups whipping cream
Dark brown sugar for
garnish**

*Use clean, uncracked eggs.

1. Line side of 9-inch springform pan with ladyfingers.

2. Dissolve gelatin in cold water. (Technique on page 15.)

3. Bring maple syrup to a boil over medium heat in small heavy saucepan. Attach candy thermometer to side of pan, making sure bulb is completely submerged in syrup but not touching bottom of pan. Continue boiling until it reaches 230°F. Pour into 1-cup glass measure.

4. Beat eggs in large bowl with electric mixer at high speed until light and fluffy. Gradually add hot syrup mixture in thin stream, beating at high speed until mixture starts to cool and stiff peaks form.

5. Stir in gelatin mixture. Refrigerate about 30 minutes or until mixture mounds slightly when dropped from spoon.

6. Beat whipping cream until soft peaks form. (Technique on page 40.)

7. Fold 3 cups whipped cream into gelatin mixture with rubber spatula by gently cutting down to bottom of bowl, scraping up side of bowl, then folding over top of mixture. Repeat until whipped cream is evenly incorporated into gelatin mixture.

8. Pour into ladyfinger-lined pan. Refrigerate 2 hours until firm. To serve, remove side of pan. Top dessert with remaining whipped cream. Garnish, if desired.

Makes 10 servings

Tropical Bread Pudding

¾ cup raisins
3 cups milk
3 eggs
1 cup sugar
1 cup shredded coconut
⅔ cup coarsely chopped
   walnuts
3 tablespoons butter,
   melted
2 tablespoons vanilla
1 teaspoon ground
   nutmeg
1 jar (8 ounces)
   maraschino cherries,
   undrained
1 can (11 ounces)
   mandarin orange
   segments, undrained
1 loaf (16 ounces)
   cinnamon-raisin bread
   Orange Sauce (recipe
   follows)

1. Preheat oven to 350°F.

2. Lightly spray 13×9-inch baking pan with cooking spray.

3. Place raisins in small bowl. Pour boiling water over to cover. Let stand 2 to 3 minutes or until plump. Drain.

4. Combine raisins, milk, eggs, sugar, coconut, walnuts, butter, vanilla and nutmeg in large bowl; mix well. Add cherries and oranges with liquid; mix well.

5. Break bread into large pieces, about 2 inches square. Add bread pieces to milk mixture. Mixture should be moist but not soupy. Pour into prepared pan. Sprinkle with additional coconut, if desired.

6. Bake 1 hour to 1 hour and 15 minutes or until knife inserted near center comes out clean. Serve warm with Orange Sauce.

Makes 10 to 12 servings

Orange Sauce

1½ cups powdered sugar
½ cup butter, melted
¼ cup whipping cream
1 egg yolk (technique on
   page 38)
2 tablespoons orange-
   flavored liqueur

1. Combine powdered sugar, butter and whipping cream in medium saucepan. Add egg yolk; mix well with wire whisk. Cook over medium heat, stirring constantly, until thickened.

2. Remove from heat and add liqueur. Let cool slightly.

Fresh Fruit Tart

1⅔ cups all-purpose flour
⅓ cup sugar
¼ teaspoon salt
½ cup butter or margarine, softened
1 egg yolk
2 to 3 tablespoons milk
1 package (8 ounces) regular or reduced-fat cream cheese, softened
⅓ cup strawberry jam
2 to 3 cups mixed assorted fresh fruit, such as sliced bananas, blueberries, sliced nectarines, sliced peaches, sliced plums, raspberries or halved strawberries
¼ cup apple jelly, melted
¼ cup toasted sliced unblanched almonds, optional

1. Combine flour, sugar and salt in food processor or blender; process until just combined.

2. Cut butter into 6 pieces; add to flour mixture. Process using on/off pulsing action until mixture resembles coarse meal.

3. Add egg yolk and 2 tablespoons milk; process until dough leaves side of bowl. Add additional milk by teaspoons, if necessary.

4. Shape dough into a disc. Wrap in plastic wrap and refrigerate 30 minutes or until firm.

5. Preheat oven to 350°F.

6. Roll dough out on lightly floured surface to ¼-inch thickness with rolling pin. Cut 12-inch circle; transfer to 10-inch tart pan with removable bottom. Press lightly onto bottom and up side of pan; trim edges even with edge of pan. Bake 16 to 18 minutes or until light golden brown. Transfer to wire rack; cool completely.

7. Combine cream cheese and jam in small bowl; mix well. Spread evenly over cooled crust.

8. Arrange fruit decoratively over cream cheese layer. Brush fruit with apple jelly. Sprinkle with almonds. Serve immediately or refrigerate up to 2 hours before serving.

Makes 8 servings

INDEX